CW00847884

Fifty Shades of Pain:

Training for the Great North Run

By

Philip Watson

Also by Philip Watson

For Adults:

Soft in the Middle

Angels in the Architecture

For Children:

The Day the Wind Blew

Harold the Bionic Hamster

Three Animals and a Baby

Twas the Squeak Before Christmas

Santa Sleeps In!

Ellie the Shy Chick.

Table of Contents

Preface

Some statistics from the WaterAid website:

'The water and sanitation crisis is the second biggest killer of children under five years old worldwide.'

'2.5 billion people in the world do not have access to adequate sanitation, almost two fifths of the world's population.'

'Around 700,000 children die every year from diarrhoea caused by unsafe water and poor sanitation - that's almost 2,000 children a day.'

Back in 2008, when I was still working in the UK Water Industry for United Utilities, I was 'suckered' into entering the Great North Run. (Just over 13 miles from Newcastle to South Shields – all uphill.)

So that someone would benefit from my pain, other than my sadistic friends, I decided to try to raise money for Wateraid – the charity of choice for anyone working in the UK Water Industry.

I wrote a diary/blog describing the pain I was going through in my training and used the updates as an excuse to email my colleagues and remind them to sponsor me.

I received a lot of positive feedback – mainly about how much they were enjoying my suffering. But it seemed to work and I raised over £1100 for WaterAid.

For some reason I did it all again in 2009.

In 2013, having just published my first full length novel, 'Soft in the Middle', on Kindle, I thought that I could use my new found publishing skills to get some more mileage out of the training diary and make some more money for WaterAid.

Now in 2018, in answer to extraordinary popular demand I have published it in paperback. I hope you find it entertaining and informative.

For more information about WaterAid, please visit: www.wateraid.org

PART ONE

THE GREAT NORTH RUN 2008

Training Diary of a 54-Year-Old Beginner

FEBRUARY 2008

It began when my sister Barbara came down for the weekend with my Mum, (or me Mam, as we like to say in the 'Real North'), and announced on Saturday morning, over a cup of tea, that it was the last day on which we could enter the Great North Run. She and her two children were applying, as were another nephew of mine and his girlfriend. The implication was clear - this could be a fulfilling and worthwhile challenge that just about the whole family could share. It would draw us closer as a family; the training would be something we could support each other in; the day of the run could be a lovely family outing!

We, my wife and I that is, had always felt inspired by the short excerpts of the Great North Run and the London Marathon that we'd seen during the BBC's comprehensive annual coverage. The runners were always having a good time and were supporting such worthwhile causes, that we felt guilty for not doing it. When you saw how old and unfit some of them were it obviously couldn't be that hard.

Every year we'd say, *'We'll* do that next year!'

Bummer! 'Next year' had finally arrived.

After only six attempts at following the easy to follow instructions on the Great North Run website, providing user name, password, likely finishing time, and, (worryingly), any physical conditions they should know about, I had registered my interest in taking part in the Great North Run. A further four attempts saw the successful registration of my wife, and by the time I registered both my son and daughter, it only took a couple of attempts.

I'm a fast learner.

At a mere £40 each to take part, and the chances of my recovering the fee from any member of family being about the same as Derby County avoiding relegation, it was obviously not going to be a cheap day out.

There was to be a draw for acceptance of applications later in the week and confirmation of the success, or otherwise, of our applications was promised by e-mail, by the end of the week.

Ideally I'd be rejected whilst the rest of the family were accepted. This would afford me the opportunity of claiming that I'd done my best, whilst not having to go through what I knew would be a long and painful training programme. Of course I'd offer them my full support in their training – helping to schedule their runs, having refreshments ready for them on their return. *Facilitating* their training rather than actually doing it.

By the end of the week my wife had received an e-mail informing her that she had not been successful. She seemed to be genuinely disappointed. I received no e-mail, so had to ring up - to find that I had been 'successful'.

Phone calls by my son and daughter revealed that they had also been successful.

I must admit, I felt quite pleased initially; after all one never likes to fail at anything; even if it is only a raffle. There's a competitive spirit that cannot be denied no matter how hard one tries. Talking of a competitive spirit I now had two offspring, much younger and fitter than I, who'd be looking forward to leaving their old man gasping in their wakes on the day of the run. (I couldn't call it a race – they couldn't beat me if it wasn't a race.) I'd have to do some serious training!

First things first though; I called in for a bottle of red wine from the supermarket on the way home. Red wine is good for the heart and I was going to need a healthy heart!

That evening over the said bottle of red – a nice subtle blend of Shiraz/Merlot/Cabernet Sauvignon/turps, a snip at only £2.99 – my wife expressed her total support and confidence in my venture.

'Are you sure you're up to it?' she asked.

'Of course I am,' I reassured her, half way through the second glass. 'I told you. I've done two half-marathons before. I probably hardly need to train.'

'That was twenty-two years ago.'

'I know that. But it's like falling off a bike. Some things you never lose. I have my natural fitness.'

'I bet you're about two stones heavier than you were; and then there's your knees.'

'Well I couldn't do it without them.'

'Right, well, you'll have to get a proper training programme and make sure you follow it. I'll come training with you if you like. It'll do me good. And I can always phone for an ambulance if need be. Our fitness campaign starts now! Any more wine?'

At work I told my manager, (sorry leader) that I was doing the run and warned everyone I met that they'd be expected to sponsor me. I also booked the day following the race run, (6th October) as annual leave.

I did consider booking the whole week off but concluded that if I were in that bad a state then I'd have to book the time off as sick leave. A lunchtime browsing on the company's I.T. system revealed an impressively comprehensive looking list of five hundred and thirty-two ailments to which I could potentially fall prone. There were a number of obvious, if alarming, possibilities that could happen during or immediately after the run: respiratory failure, heart failure, heart attack, and heart surgery, amongst others.

On reflection, these could just as easily happen during training as could many of the other conditions that were listed, such as upper back pain, lower back pain, half-way-up back pain, (not to be confused with the much more debilitating half-way-down back pain), torn ligaments and something that would become more likely as the day drew near – 'anxiety state'. The physical conditions were also ~~potential excuses~~ valid reasons for being unable to take part, and I made a mental note to revisit this list in September if the training was not going too well. I also made a note to look up Quinsy and Infectious Mononucle to check if they could be suitable, (i.e. difficult to disprove), conditions.

Obviously I no longer had a copy of the training programme that I'd used twenty-two years previously but I could remember that it was a three month programme that began with walking. I also remembered that I'd ended up wearing a knee support, although I couldn't remember on which knee. I've always had dodgy knees, (wasn't he a Greek philosopher, who founded the Cynics school?), and I knew I could expect trouble from them. I found myself a training programme by following a link on the 'GNR' – as we runners refer to it – website.

The programme attracted me because it was for beginners, and 'Day 1' was a rest day. Indeed 'Day 1' of every week was a rest day. That seemed my sort of programme. However, 'Day 2' was a thirty minute run, which I knew I wasn't ready for. The remainder of February was therefore spent making occasional visits to the gym, some of which were finished off with a walk around the two-hundred metre indoor track to get myself up to 'beginner' standard.

For some reason, at our gym they occasionally changed the direction that you had to run or walk around the track. This month it was clockwise, which was awkward for me; as an experienced armchair athlete I was used to watching people running *anti*-clockwise.

MARCH 2008

With March, came a decision to try running again; but not before I'd bought some 'proper' running shoes. Someone had recommended a shop for 'proper' runners only a few miles away, so we went there. It was quite a small shop on the High Street but at first glance it seemed to stock everything the serious runner could ever need and I felt instantly at home.

I tried on a couple of pairs of trainers and was asked to run twenty metres or so up and down the High Street in them. I was quite pleased to manage this without stopping or getting too breathless. The second pair apparently provided better support for my 'high arches', so I bought them.

I wasn't allowed by my wife, to buy any of the accessories on offer although I didn't know how I could be expected to manage without a heart rate monitor, reasonably priced at only £114.50, or a 'Power Breathe' guaranteed to increase my lung capacity for only £39.99. The 'Cybalite', which seemed to be a light to strap to one's head – a headlight in fact – to enable one to run in the dark didn't tempt me, nor did the 'Karrymore' sleeping bag, no doubt for use should one get lost if one was crazy enough to go running in the dark. My suggestion that one or both of us should invest in the Nipple Guards on offer for £7.50 resulted in a firm slap and my being kicked out of the door. Why do women always presume that a man mentioning such body parts is trying to be smutty in some way?

I suppose the juvenile giggling doesn't help.

That night I resisted the urge to go out running for miles in my new, 'proper' running shoes, and I stayed in and had some more red wine to strengthen my heart.

We visited the gym two or three times a week for the rest of the month so that I could 'break in' my new running shoes. By the end of the month we were finishing off the session with a couple of laps jogging around the track. The jogging was extremely hard work – instant pain at the bottom of my calf muscles and followed by difficulty in breathing. The track had very tight bends and short 'straights' so it felt like I was continuously running around a bend. There seemed a distinct possibility of developing a list, as there was definitely a tendency to lean into the bend slightly even at my painfully slow pace. Despite the new shoes, my knees were still hurting by the end of the month although, funnily enough, not so much while I was jogging.

APRIL 2008

April was a month of consolidation. There were still six months to go, so no need to go mad. At the gym they turned the track round so I was now running anti-clockwise like we athletes are used to. This turned out to make no difference to the speed at which I ran, nor to the pains in my legs. I did wonder if they switched the running direction occasionally to prevent people developing the "list" that concerned me last month.

By the end of the month, going to the gym twice a week, I was up to running to two and a half miles in about twenty minutes. It had become pretty boring and I'd taken to listening to my iPod. I quickly found that I had to play tracks with the right sort of beat to match the pace at which I wanted to run. If the beat was too fast then I'd run too quickly and be knackered after five minutes. If the beat was too slow then I'd still be knackered after five minutes but I wouldn't have run as far.

I was quite severe on myself this month: if I wasn't happy with my progress than I'd make myself repeat 'Day 1'! (A rest day.)

Someone at work told me about a website called 'mapmyrun' on which you can draw out your route and see how far you're running.

Cool!

I also decided in April that I would do the GNR in aid of the Wateraid Charity. There are millions of people around the world without access to clean water or to sanitation. Five thousand children die every year due to lack of sanitation whilst we complain about paying an average of one pound- a-day for all the water we could ever need and many pay more than that for just one bottle of the fancy stuff.

Hopefully people would sponsor me – to put me through the pain if for no other reason.

MAY 2008

A potential major distraction to my training this month – two weeks holiday in Fuerteventura, or 'Future Ventura' as the girl at the airport departure gate announced. However, the hotel was about a mile and half outside the resort and there was a long paved footpath close to the beach that I was determined to use to continue the honing of my natural fitness.

So, with this in mind and the fact that it was my birthday in the middle of the holiday, the present Mrs W took me off to a well-known sports shop to buy me some 'proper' running gear to go with my 'proper' running shoes. Two t-shirts made of some special lightweight material, one pair of lightweight running shorts and a pair the same length as Rafa Nadal wears - apparently Cheadle wasn't ready to see the whole length of my legs exposed - and two pairs of 1000miles running socks, whatever that means, were bought.

We flew to Fuerteventura on the tenth to stay in an "all-inclusive" hotel near the resort of Jandia in the south of the island.

Surprisingly enough I managed to stick to my plan to do some training. I ran three times each week, along the footpath that lay between the beach and the road, into the resort. On the days that I didn't run, we usually walked to the resort along the shoreline, through the huge German nudist beach – a large area of sand populated mainly by huge German nudes. It was disconcerting at first to see people walking around wearing nothing but a rucksack, a smile and occasionally a hat to protect their heads from the sun. (It seemed to me they had far more sensitive areas that were in need of protection.) And why is it that naturists on these beaches always seem to be old and overweight, and look like they need ironing?

Overall it was an excellent holiday: the hotel was very good and the food was excellent, as was the weather. There was a nice touch from the hotel – a free bottle of bubbly in our room on my birthday. This impressed my wife even after I pointed out that we were 'all-inclusive', so it was free to us anyway. It was a bit warm for running but I made sure that I was well hydrated and I thought that if I could run in those conditions then Gateshead in October would be no problem.

Then disaster struck! A couple of hours after my last run I developed an excruciating pain in my left Achilles tendon: I could barely walk. I hobbled around the hotel for the last two days struggling to get up the steps to the restaurant, ruling out any more walks through the huge German nudes. The pain eased gradually over the following days but I didn't try running again for the remainder of the month.

JUNE 2008

This was not a good month for my training. At the end of the first week I tried a short run at the gym and the pain in my tendon didn't get any worse. So I tried again a few days later but the pain hadn't got any better either. Coincidentally there was a physio at the gym giving free advice and treatment so I asked him about my tendon. He recommended not running for a while and suggested a couple of specific exercises aimed at strengthening the tendon. I took this advice and rested until the end of month. All I could really do for the remainder of the month was to look after my heart by having an occasional glass of red wine.

Red wine is obviously doubly good for you since it's simply fermented grape juice and must therefore count as one of your "daily five" portions of fruit and vegetables. The only question is whether a portion is a glass or a bottle. Either way five portions in a day is quite a challenge. I wondered what reaction I'd get a work if, instead of taking an apple out to eat at ten o'clock, I cracked open a bottle of Shiraz!

At the end of the month, Mrs W and I went out together on a two mile run. This was really a combination of walking and running since neither of us was capable of running that far. Half way round the heavens opened and we were completely drenched so that I looked like a late entry in a wet t-shirt competition- about thirty years late.

JULY 2008

At the end of the first week of July we repeated the attempt at a run. This time Mrs W's hip hurt as soon as we set off so we simply had a walk. Although we did only walk, my tendon was showing no sign of improvement and I was having serious doubts about being able to run any significant distance in the foreseeable future.

We decided to spend a weekend in Scarborough in the middle of the month, and prepared by going to M & S to buy some healthy food, (pork pies etc.) for a picnic when we arrived. Although this break delayed resuming my running for another couple of days we did walk for miles from the South Bay to the North Bay and back again, easily ten miles or more, although 'mapmyrun' said it was more like six or seven. *And* we maintained the healthy theme for the weekend by eating fish and chips on both of the evenings we were there. (You can't get better fish and chips anywhere.) I say that despite being violently sick at about half-past midnight on the second night and being hit by a strong smell of fish and chips coming back at me from the bowl. And *I* thought that vomit always smelled of parmesan cheese.

Needless to say it was another week before I attempted anymore training and even then it was only a walk to try to ease my way back into exercise. During this week of inactivity Mrs W thoughtfully bought some 'Poorly-boy' Lucozade to help me recover my energy. Unfortunately in my weakened state I managed to knock my glass over and spill it all over the lounge carpet. It turned out that it's nigh on impossible to get 'Poorly-boy' Lucozade out of a carpet and it was an insurance job.

It was around about now that I remembered that I had an ankle support somewhere that I'd bought years ago when I'd twisted my ankle playing squash. I dug this out, put it on my left ankle to support my tendon, put a knee support I found on my right knee so that both legs had some sort of support and tried a 'long run'. This went better than I had any right to expect. True, I did have pain in my tendon and my left knee but I managed to run for thirty-five minutes without stopping. Obviously that would be about four and a half miles wouldn't it? Well, not according to 'mapmyflamingrun' it wasn't; it was only three and a half. This meant that I'd actually slowed down since those early runs round the track in the gym. How could that be after all my training?

When I got home my wife, who always instructed me not to overdo it before I set out, was waiting at the door watching me struggle up the drive.

'What did I tell you?' she demanded. 'You've overdone it. You're staggering!'

'You're not so bad yourself love,' I replied.

The next day, I was at 'Day 1' of the training programme for the right reason for the first time – I'd done a long run the day before and this was a rest day! I celebrated by having a medicinal glass of fermented grape juice to look after my heart. Now that I was back on track I continued to follow the programme so the next day was a 'gentle/recovery run'. Now is this a misnomer, a malapropism, or an oxymoron? Your leg muscles and joints are still aching from your exertions of just two days ago and going out for another run and refreshing that pain before it has subsided is supposed to feel gentle and help you recover? Well it didn't! But at least I completed the run. I followed that up with another run on Thursday evening – that was three runs in one week. This run actually felt a bit easier. It was only just over two miles and I still had the pains in the usual places but I didn't feel quite as exhausted, and I could climb the stairs to the shower almost immediately when I got home!

AUGUST 2008

This was a much better month for my training. I bought another knee and ankle support so was now wearing supports on all of my leg joints and was more confident of not falling apart. During a run in the first week I even overtook a young lady on a bicycle! True, she was only about five years old and was cycling on the pavement alongside her Mum who had three other kids walking with her, but I overtook her nonetheless and she didn't 'come back at me'.

Perhaps she didn't realise we were racing.

I took to topping up my carbohydrates after a run with an ice cold bottle of reassuringly expensive lager until there were no more left in the fridge. I wasn't allowed to buy anymore – apparently they're not carbohydrates!

My long run at the end of the first week was five-and-a-quarter miles with my daughter, who would be doing the 'GNR' with me. It was reassuring to find that she wasn't running faster than me although she did give the impression that she could have run just as far again. Needless to say I was looking forward to 'Day 1' again.

I followed this with another two runs that week and realised that I was now able to run three times per week without too much worry. The pains in my joints seemed to have stabilised, perhaps due to the supports, and at the end of the week I upped the long run to 6.5 miles.

What was wrong with 'mapmyflamingrun'? It should have been at least seven miles according to my calculations.

My son arrived back from his six months' travelling round the world, and it was apparent from a run together at the end of his first week back that his plan to do some high altitude training in Peru had not materialised. At the end of a three mile run he was actually more knackered than I was. I shouldn't have been surprised I suppose. After all I was running half marathons while he was still in nappies; quite literally. He was born at the beginning of the year in which I'd run two, so he had a lot of catching up to do. He also needed to buy some 'proper' running shoes as soon as possible.

As I approached the last week or so of the month the training was going well. I was getting a new pain in my right groin as I ran but it was no worse than those in my knees and tendon and I was feeling quite optimistic. The insurance company had come through with the replacement carpet (remember the 'Poorly-boy' Lucozade incident) and that was delivered and installed one Saturday morning This meant taking the lounge furniture out and putting it back again after fitting, (with hardly any resulting damage to the doorframes), and doing the same with the furniture in the bedroom to which we had the Lucozade-stained carpet moved. To save going to the tip with the old bedroom carpet I put that down in the garage. It was a strange feeling putting the car away and stepping out of it on to a carpet. I almost felt that I should look round and check I'd not parked in the lounge. Then I mowed the lawns. All in all it was a very productive day, which I followed the next day by doing an eight mile run. The first four miles weren't too bad but the second four were very difficult. This may have been due to the exertions of the previous day or it may have simply been due to running eight flaming miles!

For the last week of the month I maintained my increasing training and finished it with a ten mile run in ninety-five minutes, which was both extremely boring and painful - but only in the usual places.

In the middle of this run I passed a busker sitting on pavement singing 'The Logical Song'.

'That's Supertramp!' I gasped.

'Thanks mate,' he replied. 'But I was going for a "smart casual" look.'

Apart from the stiffness I was feeling in my joints most days and the limp I'd developed, I definitely felt fitter and had lost at least seven pounds in weight. So I decided that after the GNR I'd try to maintain my running but on a smaller scale; about three miles, three times per week. I thought my joints should be able to stand up to that and the pains may even diminish. And anyway, a bit of pain never hurt anyone.

It was now the end of August and just over a month to go to the Great Day. If you're still reading this then it tells me two things about you:

1) You need to get out more and some interest in life – try taking up jogging.

2) Your attention span is considerably longer than mine is nowadays.

SEPTEMBER 2008

The first week of the month was a steady training week in preparation for the Sheffield '10k', on the Sunday morning. My daughter had entered herself, her brother, and me, as a good benchmark for the 'big one' a month later. My nephew also entered – a proper family outing. The youngsters stayed over in Sheffield with friends/girlfriends the night before, which was possibly not the best preparation for running just over six miles around the city.

Mrs W and I drove over on the morning itself, which was also possibly not the best preparation for running just over six miles around the city, as this involved getting out of bed at 7:00 a.m. on a Sunday morning.

Mrs W came along both to support me, and to drive back if I was incapable – forward planning that is.

I had a bucketful of pasta for my tea the evening before and topped up with more carbohydrates by having toast and cereals for breakfast before setting out for Sheffield.

Plenty of carbohydrates would apparently help me not to 'hit the wall'. I was rather thinking that watching where I was going would help me not to hit any walls. But I was leaving nothing to chance, and I'd even bought some isotonic drinks to keep me hydrated. (Mrs W said she'd stick to gin and tonic, which was quite quick for her.)

Due to my exceptional planning skills we arrived in Sheffield in good time, parked up easily and found the start by following the groups of purposeful looking people dressed in shorts and carrying sports bags. We trailed behind them, with me carrying my Morrison's carrier bag with my isotonic drinks and mini Mars Bars in it. We met up with the family at the start area and provided them with safety pins with which to pin their numbers on to their t-shirts – more forward planning. We had to assemble in groups according the background colour on our numbers. This meant that I was in group that started ten minutes after the group with the young ones in it, so we had to split up and wait for the start. Each group was taken through warm up exercises by an over enthusiastic energetic man on an elevated platform. There were two reasons why I didn't join in:

i) There wasn't room to fling your arms around and kick your legs out in all directions

ii) I didn't want to.

I contented myself with a few discrete stretches and when it was our turn, my group walked down to the start line and waited for the countdown. The run itself, an 'easy six miles', (remember I'd done ten miles the previous weekend), started in the middle of the city with a steep downhill, then ran along Penistone Road, (always gets a giggle – if it had a double "n" then it *would* rhyme with Dennis but it doesn't), to Sheffield Wednesday's ground and back again, finishing off at the top of that hill. (Somehow, Penistone Road, as is every road in the Cheadle area, is up hill in both directions when you're running along it.)

Whether it was because of the killer hill at the end or the fact that it took place in the morning and I was used to running in the evening, I don't know, but I was completely cream-crackered at the end of it. We all managed to finish it; it took me fifty-seven minutes and fifty seconds. My son won in our little group finishing in just under fifty minutes, with my nephew taking just over fifty minutes, and my daughter sixty-seven minutes. Mrs W passed this information to her parents later in the week and it became only slightly distorted when they told other members of the family, "They did ever so well; Chris won, Matthew was second and Phil was third!"

Bless!

The most exciting thing is that I was on the tele! At peak time as well; on Channel 5 at 2:00 a.m. on the Wednesday morning following the run! The cameras fortunately only caught me at the beginning of the run and not struggling along Penistone Road. Autographs are available for a small donation to Wateraid. We all managed to meet up after the race and, after a few photographs and us all failing to consume the disgusting 'energy bars' that were included in our goody bags along with our medals, Mrs W drove me home while I sipped an isotonic drink and ate a mini Mars Bar or two.

The following day was a rest day of course so I looked forward to a restful evening. But on my return home after a hard day in the office, whilst standing in the kitchen doing nothing in particular, (I'm a man, that's what we do in the kitchen), I felt a sharp, and I mean sharp, pain on the inner side of my left knee – not good news so close to the 'Run'. I didn't do any training all week and by the end of it the pain had lessened slightly and moved to behind the knee, and was really only bad when I straightened the leg out. I couldn't afford to miss anymore training and I reasoned, somewhat optimistically, and with no sound medical evidence, that since I didn't really straighten my leg while running, I may be able to train. With that in mind on the Sunday I did a relatively short run and much to my relief I got round OK, i.e. with only the usual knee, Achilles, and groin pains.

I trained as normal for the remainder of the week building up to the twelve miles run demanded by my programme at the end of it. I decided that I'd try to run for two hours and then go home from wherever I was. This was not as reckless as it sounds since my route is effectively a big circuit and I'm never too far from home. An Indian summer had arrived and it was a warm sunny morning. With this in mind I came downstairs wearing my running shorts, rather than my 'Nadal length' shorts, to help keep me cool. When she saw this, my wife promptly sent me back upstairs to put my longer shorts on. I could not be allowed out showing knee and ankle supports that didn't match! She actually said I looked like Douglas Bader.

Despite the heat and the long shorts I managed to run for two hours and ten minutes! The first hour wasn't too bad but the later stages got harder and harder and for the last half hour or so I was jobbling – a cross between jogging and hobbling. By the time I made it home all my joints below the waist were painful. There was no energy left in my leg muscles and my legs were going in all direction as I staggered up our short but very steep driveway. Twenty minutes or so later I was able to make it up stairs to benefit from the ultimate shower experience, (according to label on the bottle) provided by the wild mango and sea kelp shower gel. It obviously worked, as only 4 hours later I was able to walk around the house, though not up and down stairs, with hardly any pain.

A check on 'mapmyflamingrun' later that afternoon, confirmed that I'd run just over thirteen miles, (not the fourteen and a half I thought it should be) – I'd completed a half marathon!

The remainder of the month's training, including a six mile run at 'race pace', whatever that's supposed to mean, passed without any new pains cropping up. Not a surprise really; my body was now a temple – an ancient ruin, it's true, but a temple nonetheless. Running at 'race pace' was not a problem since I have only one pace. It doesn't seem to matter how fast I try to run it always takes me the same time to complete my route.

That effectively concludes the record of my training for the great event. I must say that I was looking forward to the day in many respects. Several people had told me what a great day it was; how great the people were, how good the atmosphere was, etc. On the other hand if I tried to run the whole way round and didn't give in to the temptation to walk then I knew that it was also going to be painful. Still it was in a good cause and I reasoned that the quicker I ran, the sooner it would be over.

The magazine they had sent me about the organisation on the day said that there was a sweep vehicle that followed on behind the runners and that if you fell behind it you had to complete the run on the pavement. Apparently it moved at seventeen minutes per mile. That's about three and a half miles an hour, so I hoped I would get a good head-start on it!

One last thing; I heard somewhere that making love is the equivalent of a three mile run. Now either I was doing something wrong or whoever said that was. After all, a three mile run leaves me exhausted and wanting to do nothing for the next hour or so... hang on a minute.

THE GREAT NORTH RUN

October 5th 2008

The Great Day!

The night before the run I stayed in Stockton at my sister's home – she whose fault it was that I was doing the run in the first place. We, (son, daughter, sister, nephew, niece and friends who were also doing the run), spent much of the evening at a pasta party at my nephew's house, where large amounts of carbohydrates were consumed in an ultimately vain attempt to store up the energy we'd need the next day. Our universal commitment was demonstrated by the fact that no alcohol passed our lips and we all retired for an early night.

The following morning, after a breakfast of a couple of bagels and a cup of tea I boarded a bus, along with the others, that would take us to our family outing. Forty minutes later we'd arrived in Newcastle and were walking through the city centre on our way to the start. I managed to drink half a litre of water on the bus and had started a bottle of 'Lucozade Sport' so that I was suitably hydrated at the beginning of the run. It was a bright sunny morning and I was going to need to have plenty of fluids 'on board' as I'd be sweating them out again later on. As we approached the start it became apparent that we all had rather too many fluids 'on board' and would have to discharge some. Fortunately there were 'Portaloos' all over the place – just one example of the superb organisation of the day.

I know they'd done it about twenty-eight times before but the organisation really was impressive. Over fifty-thousand runners and goodness knows how many spectators and everything ran like clockwork – I even had the opportunity to go the loo *twice* before the run started. At my age, once you start going....

Obviously it wasn't difficult to find the start; there were rather a lot of people to follow and we all successfully made our way to our designated starting areas, with those with the faster predicted times closer to the front. I started in the middle of the pack along with my son who had dropped back to start with me, as he'd done hardly any training due to his travelling and recent ankle injury. (Apparently running with me was the next easiest thing to not doing it at all.)

Although we were only half way back I haven't a clue how the run was started; they could have shouted 'Ready...Steady...Go!' for all I know. I heard nothing. We simply started walking forward and even started running before we reached the start line. I soon put a stop to that. There was no way I was going to run any further than I had to. The clock above the line showed that it had taken us fifteen minutes to reach the start and, after an attempt by my son to jump up to slap Tony Blair's hand, (I presume he'd started the run), we were off!

Before I get into the details of the run, (notice how I'm still not calling it a race), I'd like to say that overall it was a great day. The weather was great, the organisation was brilliant and the locals who lined the route were amazingly supportive. They were giving out ice pops, ice lollies, oranges, and biscuits. One man was standing with a garden hose spraying water into the road so that we could run through it to cool down and another was giving out free beer to the cry of, "Take away the taste of the Lucozade with some free be-ah!"

I didn't see any takers for his offer; he was standing at somewhere around the 10 mile mark and by then I couldn't be bothered to make the effort to divert to the side of the road.

Like I said, overall it was a great day. Now back to the run. It was impossible to make the common mistake of starting off too quickly, because there were so many runners. So everyone was relaxed and we all set off in high spirits - as though we really were on a fun day out. Whenever we ran under an overpass someone would shout 'Oggy! Oggy! Oggy!' and the rest of us would respond, 'Oi! Oi! Oi!'

How much fun is that?

I soon realised, that despite using the facilities twice before the start, I was still over hydrated so I to use them once again. Yes, there were loos available at frequent intervals along the course – I told you it was well organised.

It was all going very well. My son and I were running at the same pace and after a couple of miles I noticed that apart from slight twinges in my left knee and right hip. I had no pain.

This might not be so hard after all.

At one point someone shouted a warning 'Speed camera! and my son responded with the advice 'Cover your number up!' We were running uphill but it wasn't bothering us too much; it would soon level out and even start to drop. At least that's what I thought. It turned out that Newcastle must be about five-hundred meters below sea level. How the River Tyne gets to the sea I'll never understand! It's uphill all the way, apart from a short steep bit at the end.

After five or six miles of this hill, my son was a few yards ahead of me when he looked round to check on me. Rather than slow him down I waved him on and he slowly pulled away from me. I was still going reasonably well at this stage, picking my way through the crowds of runners around me. True, I had pains in both knees and ankles, but nothing I wasn't used to in training.

I jogged on and on. And the hill went on and on. I took advantage of the water and Lucozade stations as I passed them but it's not easy to drink and run at the same time and I took on little fluid in reality. But I was still going; still overtaking more people than were overtaking me. This was probably the case until about the ten mile mark. From this point on the pains were a lot worse and both hips were hurting. I got slower and slower, as did everyone around me. I consoled myself with the thought that no one in a silly costume had overtaken me. At least they hadn't until Scooby-Flaming-Doo went past me waving at the spectators!

Occasionally the children in the crowd would shout out 'Oggy! Oggy! Oggy!', but by now we were all too tired to respond, although once I felt guilty and shouted back 'Ow! Ow! Ow!'

If I thought miles ten to twelve were painful, then I knew nothing! As I stumbled down the short steep hill that led down to the final stretch and turned on to the final mile I was hardly moving.

The crowd must have been about ten deep on either side of the road and were shouting encouragement.

'Come on pet! Keep going! Not far now!'

Actually the finish was still a mile away and in my state that was a very long way. But you can't stop when there are so many people shouting you on. Especially when they're Geordies; they get enough disappointment watching their football team. I was aware that a lot of runners seemed to be overtaking me. My hips were hurting so much that I was barely able to lift my feet off the ground. I shuffled along like an old man who'd lost his zimmer frame. I passed the '800m' to go sign, and then eight-hundred meters later I passed the '400m' sign, and then after another eight-hundred meters, I passed the '200m' sign, and then finally, after another eight-hundred meters, I crossed the finish line.

And stopped.

We were encouraged to keep moving as we crossed the line to make room for the runners following, so we all staggered on in the direction of our 'Goody' bags that contained our medals, t-shirts etc. A man with a microphone pointed out that if it had been a full marathon, we'd be turning round to run all the way back. It was at this point that I realised with absolute certainty that I would never run the London, or any other Marathon.

Legend has it that Pheidippedes ran the first Marathon, from Marathon, funnily enough, to Athens to announce that the Persians had been defeated. And that having delivered the good news, he promptly died. I think I'd have given up after about seven miles and thought, 'Stuff it! They can read about it in the Daily Papyrus tomorrow!'

My time was two hours and eleven minutes, just three minutes slower than my twenty-two-year-old son, so not too bad; and it wasn't a race, so he didn't beat me.

The good news was that I'd reached my fund raising target, having raised £1100 so far; so it was worth all of the injuries and pain during training and those last few miles of the run itself.

Would I do it again next year? Are you mad?

Of course I would!

PART TWO

GREAT NORTH RUN 2009

There Must be Something Wrong With Me

There must be something wrong with me! No, it's true, really.

If you read my epic account of my training and participation in the Great North Run 2008, (see the preceding pages), you may remember, (not much memory required), that as I finally shuffled across the finishing line I swore to myself that I would never do it again. And yet only two hours later, sitting on the bus, waiting for it to take me away from the scene of torture, I was planning with the rest of the Watson Clan how we would all do it again the following year!

Now you can put that sort of thing down to the euphoria of having survived the experience, but how do you explain my actually entering the draw for the following year's run a full four months later?

OK, so my wife wanted to do it, having failed to get a place the previous year, so I really did have to enter the draw to appear to support her.

But I didn't get in!

My wife and stepson both got a place but I didn't.

I didn't have to run after all. I didn't have to go through all of that painful training.

Problem solved.

So what did I do? I wrote to the charity, Wateraid, to ask if they had any places in the run.

And of course they did.

And of course they were absolutely delighted to let me have one.

So, despite all of the pain I knew I would suffer and the difficulty in getting in, I was doing the Great North Run 2009.

I told you. There's something wrong with me.

The good news was that, despite what the media would have us believe was the coldest winter since the last Ice Age, and valiantly fighting with "man-flu" for several weeks, I did keep running over the winter. Not to the same extent as I did when I was 'in training' but enough to keep my finely tuned muscles accustomed to moving me around at something just above walking pace. I was hoping that I would reach a stage at which my knees, hips, and Achilles tendons didn't torture me every time I ran.

Unfortunately this did not happen.

So, anyway, once we were in the run officially the training had to start in earnest – an attitude of some importance.

My wife had never done any distance running and to be honest she's not really built for it – more for cooking. Still, she was extremely keen for some reason to take part in the 'GNR', and demanded that we started training immediately and I was to be her trainer. After all the years she'd spent training me the tables were turned. My wife was to become my protégé.

No sooner had she been accepted into the run that she was on t'interweb looking for suitable training guides. The good news was that she found one that advised 'easy runs' all the way up to the run in September. You may remember that I do not subscribe to the notion of the existence of an 'easy run', however, at least this guide did not demand any 'tempo running' or running at 'race pace whatever they mean, so I agreed that it looked like a very good programme.

My wife was young, (in terms of running experience) and enthusiastic, so of course we had to start training straight away. Out came my "Rafa shorts" again – I refer to Rafael Nadal and not Raphael the 16th Century Italian artist who was named after the teenage Mutant Ninja Turtle, and despite it being mid-February, the training began.

My protégé was certainly keen, although she soon came to agree that, like a 'free lunch', there was no such thing as an 'easy run' – even if it was only supposed to be for five to ten minutes. These started off as sessions combining a bit of running and a lot of walking, which gradually changed as the running lengthened and the walking shortened. February was very cold and occasionally, if there was the slightest sign of frost, I had to cancel training due to health and safety concerns.

March was a continuation of the gentle running interspersed with gentler walking, gradually building up stamina. Eventually my training started to pay dividends and we were running for over twenty minutes without having to walk. It was time to step it up to thirty minutes. The first time out my trainee managed this without a problem – how good a trainer was I?

A few days later we repeated this run but this time, just as she was finishing, my wife felt a sudden pain in her left calf muscle. There was no 'snap' - just a severe pain. Obviously she had to rest for a couple of weeks and I had to support her in that resting. Two weeks later we tried again, but the same thing happened. There was no apparent explanation for the pain, so there was no alternative but to rest for most of April.

You can imagine how frustrated I was at not being able to go out training. It wouldn't have been fair on her to have to watch me getting visibly fitter and faster while she had to rest up. April was a month of consoling ourselves that there was still plenty of time before the Great North Run and having some fermented fruit juice to numb the pain.

We started training again at the beginning of May, a mere two weeks before the Manchester 10k. I don't remember entering this but I must have done so, at the same time as the rest of the family. Needless to say, we didn't get much training in before the run - on the 17th May - as we had to take it very easy, so as not to risk injury to my trainee's calf muscle again.

Despite that we both achieved our main goals – she finished the run and I beat my stepson (by a huge eighty seconds). Apparently we ran round the Old Trafford football ground but I didn't remember seeing it! I must have been 'in the zone'.

Due to the number of participants, (about thirty-three-thousand, in this case), the runners started off at different times according to their predicted finishing times. This was done in a grossly unfair fashion. Why should Haile Gebrselassie, the greatest long distance runner of all time have been given a thirty minutes head start over me? How on earth was I expected to catch him up? I resolved not to participate again until they got their handicapping sorted out.

It was my fifty-fifth birthday only three days before the Manchester Run, so of course I was unable to celebrate, as I had to watch what I was eating and drinking very carefully. (I find I make a terrible mess otherwise.) My training also meant that I was unable to organise the tattoo I'd been thinking of having for my birthday. But never mind, I don't like bagpipes and the garden's not really big enough.

Then we were into June. You might not remember this but June was hot – at least it was when we were out running. We managed to train regularly; gradually increasing the distance we were running and decreasing the distances we were walking. We both bought new running shoes. My protégé bought them because she needed some 'proper' running shoes. I bought some because she bought some.

I managed to persuade my protégé that she was running well enough not to feel self conscious about it and that she should now be able to go out running on her own. Contrary to what you're thinking this wasn't so that I didn't have to go out training: it was so that I could run at my own pace. I found that it was more painful running at her (slower) pace than at my own, presumably because at her pace I had to take more steps and there was more wear and tear on my joints.

All in all June was a pretty good month for training. My Achilles tendon was still giving me a lot of jip but my knees didn't seem quite so bad.

Then a piggin' disaster struck – my protégé got swine flu! She was extremely ill for a couple of days and I decided that she should take at least two weeks off training – it can do more harm than good it you try to come back too soon; just ask Freddie Flintoff. Of course my body was now tuned to such a high level of fitness that the virus was unable to touch me. However, I obviously had to support my trainee in her recuperation so that was two weeks off for both of us.

By the middle of July we were off and running again, increasing the distance every week and not having to stop and walk. Strangely, just like the previous year I wasn't getting any quicker and neither was my trainee – no matter how fast we thought we'd ran a particular distance, the time was never any better. More frustrating for her was the fact that in the whole six or seven months of her training she had not lost an ounce in weight!

There's clearly something wrong with her, and not just physically – she said she enjoyed the running. That I couldn't understand. Not only was it painful it could be dangerous! Several times I'd almost been run over by cyclists, (adults, not young children), using the path instead of the road on a Sunday afternoon when they'd be just about the only traffic on the road. When did it become legal to ride a bike on the pavement?

And then there were the horses! Well not so much the horses; more what they left behind on the pavement. (And yes, what were *they* doing on the pavement in the first place?) The vast majority of dog-walkers in Cheadle Hulme clean up after their dogs and you see them walking along *swinging* their little plastic bags full of their doggie's 'business'. Not so the horse riders! Why aren't they required to clean up after themselves - and after their horses for that matter? Admittedly they'd need a big shovel and very sturdy bin bag but it was no joke hobbling round a corner to be suddenly confronted by a huge mound of horse-droppings. It's not like I could simply step over it; there was simply too much. I found that if there was someone coming the other way the best thing to do was to slow down and treat it like a roundabout.

Anyway, by the end of July the training was right back on track and on the final Sunday of the month we ran seven miles. Less than two months of this torture to go now and then I could finally hang up my running shoes, even if they were only a couple of months old.

The beginning of August was briefly marred by the realisation of my trainee that there was only seven weeks to go to the Big Day. She promptly declared that training was now serious and that we would consume no more wine until after the event! All my protestations that it was no more than fermented grape juice and counted as one of our 'daily five' fell on deaf ears. She was determined!

Fortunately her determination lasted about five days, when she adopted the more sensible approach that she would have wine at weekends only - apart from when she had some on weekdays.

Training itself went surprising well during the early part of the month. True my right Achilles was still very painful, but I'm a man so I didn't complain. The weather was a great help since, being August, it was never really warmer than 'mild' and we benefited from the occasional cooling shower. We gradually increased the 'big run' each week so that by the end of the month we were covering eleven miles – yes, in one go!

The main news of the month however, was that my company finally realised that it no longer, (did it ever?), need me and I was granted early retirement!

Now, there were obvious advantages to retiring such as not having to get out of bed until it was light, and everything that followed on from that – not getting dressed in the dark so as not wake the sleeping partner, not going to work in the dark, and not driving home in the dark.

But it was not as simple as simply not going to work anymore. You hear stories about people going to seed when they retire and going rapidly downhill. So I'd be making sure that I maintained my interests and remained active:

I'd have to keep my mind active and alert - that's what 'Countdown' was for.

And then you know how important physical activity is to me - that's obvious from this diary. Clearly I would look to maintain my interest in physical activity and renew my membership for the ~~gym~~ 'Sky Sports'.

And of course I'd have to watch what I ate as I got older but I had Saturday Kitchen and 'Masterchef' for that.

On the money side of things my income would, of course, be reduced, so I'd have to watch the pennies a bit: 'Cash in the Attic' would be essential viewing.

With so much time on my hands the demons of alcohol could become a temptation and as well as the potential health problems it could be expensive. So I'd be in the loft recovering the demi-johns and be off down to Boots to get some home brewing kits.

Some say that it can be quite difficult adjusting to the change in life style when you retire. I couldn't see it being a problem for me; I think you can see that I was prepared.

There would be changes, primarily in things I would no longer have to consider. There'd be no KPI's, no metrics, no dashboards, (apart from in my car), no scorecards, (balanced, unbalanced, or totally deranged), no traffic light reports. No core briefs, team briefs, mini briefs, Pelican Briefs. No leadership meetings, no ELTs, no SLTs, no ULTs*, only BLTs.

(*Different levels of Leadership Teams.)

No 1:1's, no interim performance reviews, no annual performance reviews, no performance ratings, no development plans, no career progression, no objectives, (SMART or stupid), no more strengths or weaknesses, (sorry areas for development).

No more insufficient bandwidth (unless it referred to insufficient bandwidth, I think it's really something to do with computers), no more going forward, no more granularity, no more stakeholder management, no more meetings, no more pre-meetings, no more post-meetings, no more action planning, socialising of ideas, and no more proofs of concept.

No, I'd have no problem in adjusting to my new jargon free environment as I went through my parallel transitional work-life balance realignment; going forward I'd simply adopt a functional, responsive, balanced, compatible, incremental, strategy to facilitate a soft landing on Planet 'Just chillin' man'.

To demonstrate my state of readiness further here are the lifestyle considerations identified in the company's pre-retirement course along with *my* answers:

How will my time be spent during the early months of retirement? **Partying**

What difference will being retired make to my immediate family / children? ***None. I'm the one retiring, not them.***

How well prepared do I feel for retirement? *I was born prepared. Why did I have to wait so long?*

What health and fitness considerations will I need to make to ensure a healthy and happy retirement? *I'll have more time to rest.*

Will I continue to work; and if so will it be part-time, self-employed or something else? *No. That's why it's called retirement.*

It turned out that my family's participation in The Great North Run was not the only major athletics event of the year. The Athletics World Championships were taking place in Berlin that month. I paid careful attention, looking for tips that could give me a valuable edge over my fellow competitors. Improving my running speed was not an option – not with my dodgy knees, Achilles tendon, hips, etc – so I focused on the different starting techniques. The fastest starts were those executed by the sprinters but I couldn't see me being allowed to take a set of 'blocks' to the start of the GNR so that one was out. I'd already tried slapping my thighs before I started like some of the sprinters did but it was far too painful. However, I did like the way the high-jumpers started their run ups. Many of them stood very still, closed their eyes and then rocked backwards and forward slightly, slowly raising their left forearm up in front of their face before launching themselves into a bouncy, bounding run up. That was the technique for me; apart from the launch into the bouncy bounding run, obviously. Before I started rocking I'd also rub my thumbs across my finger tips and then blow on them. I think I'd seen Phil "The Power" Taylor do that before he started a game of darts and if it's good enough for him....

The latter part of August was not so good for my training and I had to miss a week as my Achilles became simply too painful to run on and in fact was almost too painful to walk on at times. But my protégé made me proud. She carried on going out running on her own to the extent that she covered ten miles on the third Sunday of the month. I stayed at home and, as instructed, cooked the big chicken. Blimey that was boring! I put it in the oven and kept a close eye on it for the next one-hundred-and-ten minutes. Good job I didn't have to do the washing as well.

The following Sunday I managed to complete the ten mile course as well and I believed I noticed a significant improvement since last year. This time I had no pain in either hip, my left groin, or right Achilles tendon. Of course my left Achilles, both knees and my right groin were all extremely painful. But that's progress isn't it? Only four weeks to go. I may just about survive it. And by the time I did the run I'd be receiving my company pension.

Good grief! I'd be a pensioner.

September 1st arrived as the first official day of my retirement and with it, you'd think, so much more time for training. Not a chance. On the fridge door was a list of jobs longer than this blog – thoughtfully divided into "indoor" and "outdoor" so that the weather wouldn't slow me down.

The Sheffield 10k was on the first Sunday of the month so training was fairly light anyway. We both approached Sheffield with a degree of confidence as we'd 'put in the miles' in training – especially my protégé. However, we reckoned without the sadistic tendencies of the event organisers. You may remember from last year's account that the Sheffield run ends with a killer hill up to the finish in the city centre. Well this year I was ready for it, and whilst the run was hard, I approached the final incline with some determination. As I struggled up Yorkshire's version of the Matterhorn, you can imagine my delight as the course turned sharply left and started to go downhill. (I'd expected some sort of change as the other end of the course – at Sheffield Wednesday's ground – had turned back before rather than after the stadium.) It seemed like the run would finish on the flat! However, no sooner had I started to think about a sprint finish than the course took a sharp right and started up another steep hill. They'd put in an extra hill at the end!!

Needless to say there was no sprint finish from me although I did manage to beat last year's time by a minute. My protégé beat her Manchester time by six minutes, so we were feeling as ready as we'd ever be for the 'GNR', two weeks later.

Over the following fortnight, under my experienced and watchful eye, my protégé put some more miles in whilst being careful not to overdo it. (My other eye, the inexperienced and careless one, couldn't have been less interested.)

The weekend of the run arrived all too soon – the fact that it arrived at all was too soon for me – and we travelled up to Stockton the night before to stay with my sister, the same one who was to blame for my doing the run last year and was therefore also indirectly responsible for the pain I had gone through this time. She loaded us up with pasta on the Saturday evening and accompanied us with her two offspring to Newcastle on the Sunday to lend her support.

There were fifty-four-thousand runners this year and if I'm honest that's too many; one too many – me.

You may remember that last year I commented that the whole course was uphill, which had been a bit of a surprise as it basically runs alongside the River Tyne to the sea. This year's 'GNR' magazine once again included a cross-section of the course showing a clear downhill section from mile five to mile eight. This year I was determined to notice this section and if not enjoy it, then at least appreciate that I was not going uphill.

On the day, as always (you'll notice there is no reference to 'The Great Day' this year, as I know what to expect) the race started on time, and thousands of people ran past me shouting "Oi, Oi, Oi," in response to someone else shouting "Oggy Oggy Oggy", as we jogged through an underpass and started the long ascent to the end of mile five. It turned out to be the hottest day ever recorded anywhere on Earth – running down Death Valley would have been a picnic in comparison - so you can imagine how pleased I was to complete the first five miles and start the long downhill section.

WHAT LONG DOWNHILL SECTION?

OK, so the road did go downhill slightly for a quarter of a mile or so but then it went up again for half a mile, and then down a bit again but then went uphill even more. I was fuming and in protest, and because I was completely knackered, I actually walked up some of the uphill sections. After all, they weren't supposed to be there, so why should I run up them?

It really was surprisingly warm so I was extremely grateful for the water stations and did manage to keep taking on fluids. When I reached the final mile along 'the front' at South Shields I think I actually managed to speed up slightly, and eventually staggered across the line in a time of two hours and sixteen minutes. This was about six minutes slower than last year, which I put down to the extremely high temperatures, (somewhere in the region of 40ºC) and the fact that I was suffering from bursitis in my left elbow. That's inflammation of the bursa to you non-medical types; so I think my little white blood cells were dashing around fighting that instead of pushing my legs along. But I'm a man so, as you know, not one to make excuses. I was even more tired at the end than last year and couldn't manage to take the top off the bottle of water I was given at the end.

My protégé made me extremely proud by finishing in two hours and forty-four minutes – shows what a good trainer I am. My daughter finished in two hours forty minutes despite being stopped to give an interview, (which wasn't shown on tele) and my son came in under the two hours' mark at one hour fifty-seven minutes.

We had had the foresight to take our mobile phones with us so that we could find each other more easily after we'd finished. Of course they didn't help at all as there were fifty-four-thousand other people trying to use their phones as well, so it was just about impossible to get through. Still we obviously found each other eventually and hobbled back to the bus.

The previous year it had been whilst waiting for the bus to leave that we all agreed to do it again this year. You'll be wondering if the same this happened this year.

No, it didn't.

Whilst my time this year was six minutes slower than last and about thirty-nine minutes slower than my best of twenty-odd years ago I still claimed it as a 'PB' for me – a Pensioner's Best.

And that seems a pretty good note on which to retire permanently from half marathon running.

I hope you've enjoyed reading this a damned sight more that I enjoyed running although I appreciate that you've needed almost as much stamina.

If this has inspired you to take up half marathons then you've missed something and I suggest you read it again!

THE END (for now)

Printed in Great Britain
by Amazon